SECRETS IV:
Amusing Grace

Dr. Bob Woodard

Enjoy

Bob & Darla

SECRETS IV: Amusing Grace

Copyright © 2019 by Dr. Bob Woodard

ISBN 9781073339099

~

Cover illustrator
Darla Hudson Woodard, CZT
Certified Zentangle Teacher & Artist

Table of Contents

DEDICATION

To Mom and Dad and Brother Rich
who got me off to a great start in life.
Now gone, but good company still

INTRODUCTION

This is the fourth book in this fascinating series called *SECRETS*. In a poetic style, Dr. Bob's presents a whimsical observation, a short story or a thought provoking insight in only a few well-crafted words. These 100 poems are easy reading and tap into our own experience in a way that makes it hard not to read the entire book in one sitting. The ending of each poem is often surprising making us curious about where the next one will take us. The author was a psychotherapist, who considered it a privilege to have shared in the lives of over 5,000 clients during his career. His experience has acquainted him with life's many surprises, challenges and triumphs. It tells of the everyday, ordinary secrets we may or may not have shared.

The title of this book includes the phrase, amusing grace. It reflects his fascination with the many ways with which we have been graced to see life situations and the power we have to choose to see tragedy or humor, horror or hope, hell or heaven.

You will have a hundred experiences as you read this often amusing and uplifting book. Much of it touches on our common search for happiness, romance, purpose and meaning. You will find everyday characters, humor, inspiration and the strength that comes from taking a chance on love and life knowing it will change and deepen us.

Poems can keep us company for a lifetime. Since they can be read and reread, they are a gift that keeps on giving and as we grow they take on new meanings. Enjoy the experience.

1. INSIDE SECRET

Secrets
Are often about relationships
The covert
Hidden ones

But I
Was thinking about
My relationship
To myself

No one ever asks me
How that's going

How're you getting along
With yourself

It wouldn't make sense
To them
Or it might be too personal

If someone knew
How I was getting along
With myself

They might try
To match me up
With someone
Else
Inside
A nicer self

One who would treat me better
Honor and appreciate me
More

Maybe
I should consider it

2. EXPECTATIONS UNMET

You've met them

They had lovers
Parents
Children
Brothers or sisters
Who didn't meet their
Expectations
And broke their hearts

They suffered
For decades

Perhaps your heart
Stayed broken
In this way

Until you finally
Released
Your
Unrealistic
Unmet
Heartbreaking
Expectations

So your heart
Could heal
Unexpectedly

3. DON'T RAIN ON MY RAIN

Hey
Not so fast
I don't want to leave the past
I still want to tell you
My story

I want to dwell
On the pain
Again and again

I need to drag it out
I need to cry and shout
About it

Console me
And tell me they were wrong

I'm so mad, I'm so sad
All the trouble's been so bad

Just sit and listen 'til I'm done
Can't you see I'm upset
It's painful
And a weird kind of fun.

4. LEFT OUT

Everyone wants to be right
Not left

Be right on
Not left off
Or left out

Be Mr. Right
No one's ever heard of Mr. Left

Don't be out in left field
Left-handed
Left on base
Or left behind

To be left
Just doesn't seems to be
Right

5. LOVE SHOWED UP

Love showed up today
In a way
Unexpected
As it often does

A thank you note
An "Hello"
And cookies from a neighbor
I didn't know

Love showed up
Today
As it always does
In a way
Unexpected

As a cup of tea
Made for me
Perfectly by Darla

Love showed up
Unexpectedly
Today
In a way
As it always does

As a memory
Of my brother
My father
And my mother

6. MY BEST FRIEND

I rose today
So I could play
With my best friend

I should say
I spent yesterday
The entire day
With her

She fascinates me
I must say
She responds
To my every touch
In a special way

Someday
In the future
She'll go her own way
Soon to be forgotten
But it's o.k.

When she's gone
Others will say
Something even better
Was on its way

Probably
The one who took her away
Will take her place

And she will say
My friend
That old I Pad
Has had her day

7. UNNOTICED POWER

The power of letting go
A strange notion
I know

It would seem easy
To release
To open
A hand
A mind
A heart

To exhale
To breathe again
To start
Fully present
Ready for the day

Having let go
In our own way
Of what was

Or wasn't
Here to stay

8. TIMELINES

Where are the lines of time
Do they stretch out before us
Or behind us

Are they filled with child-like
Anticipations
Or reveries
Of moments past

Will they last

Are the lines drawn on our faces
Or on the map of places we've been
Or wish to see

In time
We choose
The places we can be
Instead of now

Time lines draw us forward
Or backward
Becoming our favorite dwelling places

In time

9. HEALING THE LONGING

When he felt safe with me
He said

Something is missing
I don't know what to do

I said
Ask for a healing

What

Ask for a healing

What do you mean
What do you think
Would be healed

Your Divine discontent
The open wound
The sense of longing
For what you need
At the deepest level

What do I need
At the deepest level

If you ask
If you open

If you stop resisting
The healing of your
Discontent
The answer
Will come
And you will be healed
In a way you cannot know
Until you ask

How will I know
I am healed

Others will know
You have found contentment
And when they feel safe
They will say to you
Something is missing
And you will tell them
To ask for a healing

10. HAPPY TRAILS

Was it possible

He left a trail
Of happiness behind

People thought of him
And smiled

He was fun
Full of energy
Ideas
Activities

And love
Freely given

Remember

11. MORNING JOY

You will have joy
In the morning
When you arise
With eyes truly open

Singing
As the birds sing
To greet the new day

You will have joy
In the morning
When you arise
With your heart
Full of gratitude

Embracing
All that
You truly love

You will have joy
In the morning
When you arise
Full of hope
And
A plan
To play
Your way
Through this
Fun-filled day

12. WELCOME WORDS

Nancy said:

As I stood
On my surfboard
I surged on the wave
Feeling out of control
Moving directly
At those little children

I saw the frightened
Look on their faces
As I yelled for them
To get out of the way

The danger
Consumed me
With fear

Then
Somehow
I remembered
The profound words
Of my teacher
Surfer dude

"You'll go
Where you are
Looking"

Shifting my view
From the children
To the shore

I felt the magic board
Beneath me
Changing direction
Taking me away
From danger
To the safety of the beach

13. UNAVOIDABLE CHOICE

Yes, I know
He began doing something he loved
Only to discover later
It harmed
Him
And those who
Loved him

But he couldn't stop
Himself
Alone

So he made the easier choice
To hide it
To do what he loved in secret
When no one could see him
'Cause he wanted to protect himself
And his choice
And the way he was
Or had become

But secrets always escape
Their dark hiding place
It's their nature
To seek the light

Once exposed
Secrets bring us back
To the only healing choice
To let go of a love that hurts us
And move on
To the love that heals us

14. TELL A HEALING STORY

You don't know why it happened
But it hurt
And you cry
And you want to know why

It tore you apart
It broke your heart
And now
Where to begin
Where to start

So you go back in time
To try to make it unhappen
With stories of misunderstanding
And conflict

Stories that make you sick

So
Instead
Begin to tell a story of healing
See the hidden force of grace
Behind it all
That set you both free
Tell of the grace in him
And in you
And all that you now see

Tell a story that heals you
And each other

Letting go of your own misery
And his

Tell a story of what is to come
Tell of your healing
And your new found freedom
To see
To love again
To be now
And what you want to be

15. DREAM WATCHER

Did you ever notice
How dreams come true
You'll notice them more
If you keep them in view

Today you will marvel
As more dreams come true
Small and large
They'll be more than a few

Some took time
Some even grew
Some happened once
 Some are overdue

Remember the past
When your dreams
Led you fast
To the future
You wanted

If you notice

It's true

Dreams give direction
Delights to pursue

Creating a vision
A new way to see
What you will do
And who you will be

16. THE EMPTINESS

On the warm moonlit evening
The study group completed
We stood outside the church
Sharing our insights

Eileen, who sought a healing
Thru Al Anon
Mentioned her pain-filled childhood

She said
You know, Bob
You had a happy childhood
You don't know
"The Emptiness"
People like us feel

Maybe she was right

'Though I'd spent decades
As a therapist wanting to help
How could I really know

Yet
I had come to understand
How emptiness is
Born in mistrust
The unpredictable
And a misdirected
Search for safety
Not love

When love is scary
It is hard to surrender
To the reciprocating love
Of God, ourselves and others

Some choose to know
Only emptiness
The familiar
When the love that surrounds them
Doesn't feel safe
Yet

17. SANDY BORN AGAIN

She said
When he left
It was like death

My death

I was thrown
Into a new life
Born again

Not knowing
Where I was
Or
Who I was

Crying at each
Frustration
Not knowing
Who was taking
Care of me

I did not know how
To reach for
What I needed

Or how to put into words
What I felt

It was as if
I had to learn to
Walk again
To find a way
To get to what I needed

I kept falling down
But getting to my feet
Again
Over and over

And then I began to see
I really was born again
I was alive
Not dead

And I had a new life to live

18. KEYS TO THE FUTURE

He closed the door
On his future

From inside
He locked it tight
With his keys

Then he went to the window
Of his fifth story apartment
Opened it wide

With all his keys
In hand
He tossed them
Out the window
Out of his life

He watched them fall
All the way to the sidewalk
Just missing the man below
And watched them bounce

The man on the sidewalk
Looked down
Picked them up
And without looking
For their source
Put them in his pocket

Now
From the fifth floor
Suddenly confused
He watched the man below
Walk away with the keys
To his future

19. THE APPEARANCE

She found herself
Alone
At the back
Of the filled concert hall
In the rock-concert atmosphere
She could feel
The expectancy of the crowd
Now growing impatient

The stage was empty
Where was He
He was late
When was He
Going to show up
Where was God
The star of the show

The standing crowd began to chant
We want God
We want God

She could see the stage
And began to work her way
Toward it
Through the high-energy crowd

After squeezing her way
To the front
She reached the stage

And looked up
Looking for God

Somehow she realized
He wasn't
Ever going to appear
On this stage

Then
She heard a voice
From her side
Slightly behind her
Saying
I am here
I have always been here
Right by your side

She teared-up
And together
They left

Her prayer answered

20. IS IT SAFE

Is it safe
To share your
Softer thoughts
With those you love

Is it safe
Not to

Is it safe
To share your
Seeking
With those you love

Is it safe
Not to

Is it safe
To share your
Passion
With those you love

Is it safe
Not to

Is it safe
To share your
Secrets
With those you love

Is it safe
Not to

21. UNREQUITED LOVE

This is the love
Just out of reach
That temptation
That unending obsession
With the love
That would complete us

If only he
Or she
Would surrender
Letting go of all others
For me

Possessed by an absence
Seeming to be present
But only in fantasies
Fulfilled

Yearning for what is
Missing
We are consumed
By what is not
Present

While the love
That is
Goes unnoticed

22. THOUGHT FREE

It is not life I hate
Or find hard
Or unbearable

It is not injustice
I despise
And loathe

It is not those people
Who disgust me

It is my thoughts
That have ruined my joy

Ladies and gentlemen
Of the jury
I am innocent
I did not know
The source of my unhappiness

No one told me
Until
It was almost too late

And when I was told
I was choosing these thoughts

I didn't believe it
At first

Not really

And now I tell you
I was innocent then
And I believe it

But now
Knowing
I had been choosing
The very thoughts
That made me unhappy
I was set free
To savor the joy of living

23. THE ROAD TO DOUBT

When you take
The road to Doubt
You believe
It's the one way out
Of Faith

The road to Doubt
Takes you out
Not in
Looking
Hereabout
Thereabout
Roundabout
Still without
The guide
The faith full talk about

And on your way
To Doubt
You whine and pout
And sometimes
Even scream and shout
Believing there is
No way out of Faith
Except to go to Doubt

Once there

There's no way out of Doubt
But in
To doubt your Doubt
And let your trip
To Faith begin

Again

24. CHILHOOD REUNION

Darla told me
About her experience at lunch
With a long-ago-friend
From the past

She said
We knew each other
As children
Our fathers were friends
Co-workers
Our families intermingled

Until his father died
Then
It was too painful
For him
To see me
Anymore
That's what I always thought
That's what I always wondered

Forty years later
Here we were
Meeting in Reno
For lunch

As we remembered
Together

It took us back
To that day
To that park
The place
In San Luis Obispo
In the fifties
To our childhood

We were innocent
The only time
When we were able to be kids

Just before his father died
And left him
To a life he didn't expect

And before my father
And the woman
Who loved me
Broke up
My life

And Dad sent me away
To a mother
I never knew-
At lunch...
We both went back
To that town
Looking for our childhood
Still

But all we saw
Were these strangers
Adults
Stepping on the memories
Of what we had
So briefly

A childhood
That disappeared
When our
Little bodies
Started being adults
And play was left behind
In a moment
We shared
From our past

25. POWER

Power
Pours out of purpose

It is the organizing
Unifying
Force

It is the alignment
Of thoughts
Energy
And resources

It is direction
Discipline
And focus

It is the overcoming
Of distraction
To accomplish
A goal

We can use
Such power
For good

Or
Not

26. SETTING MYSELF FREE

I am of an age
When I don't care
How much I share
Or if you think I'm crazy

I confess
My rebellion
I guess
Of the inner kind

When I was small
I so recall
I hid it all
Inside

As if my safety
Lie in being shy

For joy and
Spontaneity
Was truly not
The thing to be

Or so
My little self
Thought
Better to be
Not
Me

Rather reserved
Repressed
And so
Suppressed

But now you see
I no longer care
To go on hiding
Me

27. PEOPLE DON'T CHANGE

People don't change
He said
To keep himself
Safe
So he wouldn't
Fall in love with her
Again
Back into the
Soul sickness
Of trying to make
The unworkable work

After all she was
Flawed
Unworthy
Of the risk

He couldn't trust
Himself
To consider
The possibility
Change might bring

She might have
Changed
Her thinking habits
Her unhappiness habits
Her habits of mood

Too dangerous a way
To think about her
After all these years
Of letting go

And changing
His thinking habits
His happiness habits
And
Habits of mood

28. GIVING

Life is about
Thanksgiving
And gratitude
For everything
Everyone and
Every resource

Life is about
Forgiving
As we stop picking
At old wounds
So they can heal
And our attention
Can shift to other
Passions and people

Life is about
Gift giving
Sharing our talents
Our love
And our pleasures
With ourselves
And others

Life is about
Giving up
Our misgivings
Learning to trust
Our joy and happiness

Life is about
Giving in
To giving

29. RICH

When I was little
And Mom was rushed
Or in a hurry
She called me
"RichBob"

Rich was my older brother's name

As I look back
I was indeed
Rich
Because of all
He gave me

He led me
Into sports, appreciating music
His same four part-time jobs
Youth groups
And college
We were even roommates in
Graduate school

Later in life
He was amused
By my desire to follow him
Down a path he made so easy

I don't think he realized
The great experiences

He led me to
Along the trail
We traveled together
For twenty years

Thank you precious brother
For leaving me
Rich...Bob

30. GENERATIONAL GOALS

Out of his poverty
And his pain
Dad set goals
For himself

Be responsible
Value people
Contribute to their wellbeing
And
Take care of your family

But one goal
Went unmet
He left it
Part of our inheritance
To my brother and I

The desire
To complete
A formal education
And college

That was what
We were to do

My brother figured out
How and where

And so we did it

And Dad
Still smiles
At our/his accomplishment

31. DOG WARS

Months ago
The invasion started

Large sound bombs
Began penetrating the house
Landing everywhere

Unpredictable
Day and night

Launched
By a neighbor
His dog
Sound Blaster
Out of control
Violating every
Neighborly boundary

Breaking the
Sound barrier
Of peaceful coexistence

Yet the neighbors
Suffered
From their own silence
Without barking back

Scared of
The Big Dog
Owner

Who was
Scared of
Stopping
His scared dog
From barking

32. FINDING MY WAY

What do I want

Or better still

What is the
Experience
I seek
As my will
And Thy will
Join

This question
Guides me
As I move away
From pain
And the ordinary view
Of things
That leads me to complain

So often I ignore
The power
Of this question

And I strain
Against direction
And remain
Unwilling
To gain
From my connection

Then noticing
My sense of loss
And my aloneness
I surrender
Again

To ask the question
That gives direction
To my journey
From resistance and resentment
To excitement and contentment

What is the
Experience
I seek
As my will
And Thy will
Join

In the moment
Of co-creation

33. WALKING SENSATIONS

A simple walk
A simple act of pleasure

A quiet mind
Seeing without comment

Noticing the experience

I walk

Merged
With my surroundings

Concept free
Sensation filled

Enjoying the motion
Of each stride

I walk
I simply walk

34. THE DWELLING HABIT

Who we are
Is a dwelling habit

We dwell
On our sadness
Our fears

We dwell on
Our anger
Or our happiness

And this is who
We become

Others come to
Know us by
Our mood

And they stay
With us
Or go away

Depending
On theirs

35. HAPPY LANDING

We were landing
In Sacramento
A surprise

After all
We thought
It would be Reno
'Til
The weather turned bad

No point
In getting mad

I was glad
The pilot
Had advisors
Rules
Regulations and policies
All lined up
To decide not
To risk our lives
By landing
In blinding snow

Despite the grousers
How loud they grow

You know
When surprised

In Sacramento
Now I looked ahead
Glad to be here
Rather than in Reno
Dead

36. LISTENING

TO MY OTHER SELF

I thought I was
A victim
Of your point of view
But the truth
Was long overdue

For so long
I thought I was wrong
And you were right
And strong

Trapped in
Your sadness
Your worry
And madness

 I was unsure
Thinking
I could endure
What you said
And
Who you were

I was quite unaware
That in your despair
You wouldn't care
What effect
You were having

On me
By the negative
Way that you see

You may think
I'm upset with you
But it was me

'Cause I listened
Much too carefully
And took on your identity

Not realizing
I was not you
And you
Were not
Me

37. LIFE IS NOT

Life is not
A problem
To be solved
An obstacle
To be overcome
Or
A responsibility
To be endured

It's an experience
To be enjoyed

So tempting
It is
To make it
Hard
Not soft
Complicated
Not simple
Closed
Not open

What would it be like
What would you do
Who would you be

If your life was fun

38. KIM

How blessed
I am to have
A daughter
Who is so blessed

Full of talent
Full of love
That overflows
To friends
And family

And flows back
Through Peter
A loving husband
And a home
Full of loving
Dogs and birds
And such a
Spirit of welcome

How blessed
I am to have
A daughter
Who blesses me

Someone dear
A special friend
Wise and clear
About what matters

39.   MOVING ON

PAST THE MIDDLE

Don't go away
Stay
I have some things
To say to you
About yesterday
And your tomorrow

When I was younger
About your age
At a different stage
Of my life

Sandwiched in the middle
Between
Independence and
Dependency
Young and old

It was a time of responsibility
And job identity
When my young
Were moving on
And my old
Were slowly moving on
Toward the next life

And I carried the weight
And worry of these goodbyes

And the sighs of change
That eventually set me free
Of all this generational
Responsibility
While their love remained
With me

As I moved on
To a different life
That was once
Too far in the distance
To have dreamed of

40. OPENINGS

I had been
Walking my little dog
After dark
And was returning
To the entry way
Of my gated community

A young man
Was standing before
The locked automated gate
Which was activated
By a remote key

He had two plastic bags of groceries
One in each hand
And he was swinging them
Around with each arm

I watch from the shadows
Realizing he thought it took
Vigorous motion to activate
A motion detector that would open
The gate

There was no motion detector
And the gate was not opening

Amused
And still undetected

In the shadows
I pressed my remote button
And the gate opened
For the young man
And he went in

I imagined his confusion
When the gate didn't open
The next time he flailed his arms
At the entry gate

Sometimes we get help
From unknown sources
And a closed door opens
Without our knowing
How or why

41. RESISTANCE

I once had a car
I was fond of
Or
Should I say
I was used to

It ran
Just fine
When I was going backwards

But when I tried
To move forward
The emergency brake
Would engage
Slightly

At first I hardly noticed
It was subtle
But I could feel
Some resistance
Whenever I tried
To go ahead
To my destination

It was draining
At the time
And I didn't know
The cause

But I talked
With my father
Who identified
The problem
But I never got it fixed

I thought the car
Wouldn't like me
If I didn't drive
With my emergency brakes on
The way it was used to

For that matter
That's the way
I got used to traveling
Why change

What would you
Have me do

Release the brakes
Completely

I'd miss the resistance

42. FISHING FOR THOUGHTS

In our mind
Is a stream
Of thoughts

We need a filter
A net
To bring in
The big ones
While letting go
Of the little ones

We want to select
A meal
For the mind
That will
Nourish our bodies
As well

Not every fish
Is worth catching
Most can be thrown
Back into the stream
Until they grow up
Or just move on
Out of our stream of
Consciousness

43. TOO TALL AND TAKEN

When Donnie
My best friend
And I were eight
We were smitten
With our classmate
Karen

She was blonde
And beautiful
And tall

Even at that age
We knew
The difference
In height
Was too big a barrier
To be overcome

When you're that young
Love between the sexes
Means
You get to look at someone

By the time Donnie
And I were ten
We wanted to see where
Our princess lived
So we followed her home
From a distance

At the time
It was a daring adventure

In fifth grade
Our fantasy girl
Disappeared
Although nobody
Told us why or where
She went

I always wondered

When I was nineteen
A miracle happened

She reappeared
In a hospital
Where
I was a hospital orderly
And she was a nurse's aid

Now we were work mates

Still blonde
And beautiful
But now short enough
To look up to me

I was hopeful
'Cause I happily met
The height requirement

And our meeting
Was a match

But
She was engaged
Unavailable
Still
And forever

Except in my
Little boy mind

44. UNOPPOSED

What if
Just for today
I stopped opposing
My own thoughts

What if
Just for today
I completely
Allowed
The weather to
Be
My to-do list to
Be done
And
The behavior
Of other drivers to
Occur

What if
Just for today
I failed
To see danger
In a difference
Of opinion

What if
Just for today

My encounters
With everything
Were interesting
Rather than slightly
Annoying

What if
Just for today
I left myself alone
Unquestioned
And unopposed

45. THINGS THAT HIDE

Why do we play
This game of
Hide and go seek

You know
The three things that hide
To teach us a lesson

When we can't
Find our slippers
We have cold feet
Without our glasses
We are blind
Without a pen
We can't remember

Slippers
Glasses
And pens
They hide

Then they show up
As if they were there
All the time

And claim
They were never hiding

46. UNDYING QUESTIONS

Why do we rely
On the fear
Of death
Not the love
Of life to
Keep us alive

Why does it
Go unnoticed
That the fear
Of life
Keeps us dead

Why are zombies
So interested in
Ending life

And the living
So interested
In zombies

Why are we so fascinated
With the living dead
But
With the living and loving
Not so much

47. AT WAR WITH MYSELF

I used to start
My day
Resisting right away

My tools
Of self-torture
Are here
On display

Here is my timeline
My to-do-list
And goals

Once I set them
For the day
I began to regret them
And wished they'd
Be taken away

I began to resist
Even while I insist
They all must be done
And on time

So one part would
Whine
And be stressed
While the other would say
Are you doing your best

You can see
Right away
How I spoiled my day
In this strange sort of way

At war with myself

48. MY DWELLING PLACE

No one
Had to tell me
To dwell on fear
Or anger
Or even sadness
I was good at it
Just like you are

It was automatic
By the time
I reached the age
Of reasons

'Cause I'd
Made up all
My reasons

But now I know
From a good
Source
Rather
I was meant to dwell on happiness
Joy and gratitude

To practice wallowing in
Savoring
Reveling on

And extending
My communion with
Joy

This is my dwelling
My holy place
My meant-to-feel
Experience of
God's presence

49. FINDING YOUR

SOUL MATE

What if the one
You were seeking
Were inside

This one
Who recognized
Your essence
Your beauty
And the wonder
That you are

What if the
Union
And communion
That you are seeking
Were found

And your longing
And your loneliness
Disappeared

What if
Within you
Is the one
Who is seeking you
To find completion
And together

Be
The overwhelming
Co-creating
Love of your life

50. HELEN'S SECRET

Helen
Finally asked herself
Why
She did not share her love for Him
With others

Or even
With herself with herself

For years
She kept it a secret

She thought it
Would make her look
The fool
And lose the respect
Of the professional cynics
Who were in her life

Why He came into
Her life and changed it
So profoundly
Did she still pretend
He wasn't real
Or really there

And now
She finally asked Him

His answer
Brought her to tears

He said
You are ashamed
Of Me

And she knew
What He said
Was the painful
Truth

51. LETTING GO

When you let go
Of fear
A secret world
Will appear

It is the experience
You always wanted

When you let go
Of your bitterness
You will know
A world of sweetness

It is the experience
You always wanted

When you let go
Of the things that have
Already left you
You will know freedom

It is the experience
You always wanted

When you let go
Of fear
What stand in your way
Will disappear

52. BLAMLESS

Some parents
Don't live the life
They want
So they can provide
That life to their children
It would be the life
They wished they had

Some children
Don't live the life
They want
So they can provide
That life to their parents
It would be the life
They wish their parents had

Some other parents
And some other children
Lived the life they wanted
And they are pleased
To have shared that life
With each other

53. PENANCE

One day I was alone
At the park
In a small grove of elm trees
A block from my house

I was very present
Viewing
The details of nature
Enjoying
The solitude
Of the moment

I picked up a rock
As a boy of twelve
Will do

I noticed a small bird
About to take flight
So I threw the rock
And
To my amazement
Hit and killed it
In midair

Suddenly
I felt only grief
For taking
The life of this little bird

A few moments later
A big friendly boxer
Appeared from nowhere

He came over
To greet me
And lean against me
As I began to rub
His large head and ears
I felt some consolation
And comfort
Given what I had done

And then
I felt the warmth
Of a stream of liquid
On my leg
Soaking my jeans

Surprised
But somehow
Relieved
Was I too

That the animals
Had expressed
Their opinion
And offered
The penance
I seemed to need

54. THE UNVEILING

Beyond the veil
Lies the unknown
The illusive reality
We cannot see

I always thought
The veil
Was placed
There by God

But
We place the veil
Between us
And
The mystery
We call God

Veils
Also
Hide us from one another
And the beauty
We would see
That would compel
Us to union

We fear the power
Exposure
And
Self-revelation would bring

Long ago
Men thought
The veiling of women
Would protect them
And theirs
From the impulse
To love

And
Among themselves
Women thought
Men were also veiled
Not to hide their bodies
But to hide
Who they were

Veils
Will disappear
When we discover
The Love we seek
Lies behind
Our own veil

55. PEACE OF MIND

Pausing
In a moment
Of self-reflection
Perry said

My mother told me once
Or perhaps many times
Stop talking Perry
You don't have to share
Every thought
That crosses your mind

When I did
Stop chattering
She became peaceful
In my presence

Now
When my own mind
Is filled with self-chatter
I remember her words
Stop talking Perry

And
I become peaceful
In my own presence

56. WILL ANY THOUGHT DO

I care for him
Very much
But as I began drowning
In his monologue
Of random thoughts
That made him unhappy
I asked him
If he ever considered
Choosing the best of his thoughts

Curious
About my question
He said
Not really
Why do you ask

I told him
I believed choosing your best thoughts
Was the secret
To a happy life

He said
I think
It would be boring
And besides
It would be unnatural
To choose your thoughts

And
What about being spontaneous

Well
I said
Not every thought
That surges through my mind
Is worth my attention

Only a few lead me to the
Life I want to live and enjoy

I've given up
Being a victim
Of my thoughts
Most of the time

Now I choose the ones
That create a feeling
Of gratitude and happiness

And it works

He said
It sounds too simple

And
Carefully
Selecting my thoughts
I said
It is simple

He said
That's easy for you
To say
You're happy

57. NEW YEAR'S EVE

Gratitude moments
For the passing year
And what was

I remember who blessed
My life
Bringing love into it

I remember
To whom
I expressed some love
In loving ways

I remember
The passion
Interest
Creation and
Activities
I shared and enjoyed
In a childlike way

I remember
The new ways
I loved and took care of myself

And
I remember
The moments I spent
In the Presence of God

58. UNKNOWN PROTECTION

You don't know
My name
But I'm here
To resist

To keep you
The same

Let me explain
I'm here to help you
Refrain
From stressful things
That might tempt you
Again

I am here to say
No
When you want to go
To play or enjoy your day

I want you to stay
To close your eyes
Avoiding open doors
And goodbyes

Hoping' you won't
Take chances
When you exchange
Glances

With opportunity

Can't you see
In all sincerity
I'm here to stop you
From experiencing
The unknown
And change

To keep it away
To keep you safe
Every single moment
Of every single day

59. ONLY ONE REHEARSAL

This time
It was a conflict
Over the barking dog
Of a neighbor
Who lived behind me

As I walked in a park
I found myself
Getting ready
For the drama

Me
Playing both parts
Telling him
What he was doing wrong
Ready to respond
To any counter point
He might make
About how I was wrong

On and on
For so long
This imaginary
Rehearsal went on

As I walked
Over and over
In my fury
I would come up
With clever comebacks

To things he would never say
Then tired of the fighting
I realized
He wasn't there in my head
It was my own two-headed
Argument with me
A victim of my own head banging
Against itself

How could I stop this headache

For relief
I created a holy commandment
For myself
One Rehearsal Is Enough

As I found myself
Rehearsing the imaginary argument
Again
I interrupted it
Saying
Rehearsal's over
One Rehearsal Is Enough
And the argument
Stopped

60. MOOD STAINS

Your worry got on me
Yesterday
And I wanted to know
How to get it off

It must have happened
When I rubbed against you
And it stained my happiness

It's not your fault
Mine seems to pick up moods
Whenever I get close

Were you able to get it off
Has it disappeared yet

If yours is gone
Let me know
So I can relax
Knowing it disappears
Or fades
Over time

61. HEALING

Healing
What is it
We want healed

Our relationship
Ourselves
Our hurting

What prevents our
Healing
Anyway

Perhaps
It's the story
We keep telling about
The separation
That should never have happened

Perhaps we
Need to tell
The story
Of our healing
Instead
Of the story
Of our hurting

So healing
Can be
The real story

62. THE STORY UNCOVERED

As my wife and I
Drove her home
The woman said
From the back seat

Your know
The story I have to tell
Is important
But I find myself
Hesitating
I'm not sure I want
To share it so publically

I said
You remind me of what
Edna St. Vincent Millay
The poet
Once said

A person who publishes a book
Appears willfully in public
With his pants down

You know
She said
You've got me thinking
My kids are off to work
During the day
Maybe I'll try writing that way

You know
With my pants off
It might be just the thing
To set me free
To finish writing my story

63. DREAMS UNENDING

This morning
I noticed
For the first time

Dreams
Don't have endings

For that matter
They don't have beginnings
Either

Dreams
Seem always to start
In the middle of an experience

We are lost
Falling
Flying
Having sex
Trapped
Chased
Unable to move
Or escape

And then
We awaken

Even if we
Go back into the dream
It is never ending

Perhaps
The purpose of the dream
Is to awaken us

64. TEARS OF RECOGNITION

Why are we moved to cry
When someone we love
Is officially appreciated
In public

What is it
That wells up
Within us

Is it gratitude
That gently seeps from
Our eyes

Is it the delayed release
Of a group's love
Gone unexpressed
Too long

Is it that our private love
Is expressed eloquently
For us

Or is it
The open recognition
Of one person's specialness
When we doubt
Our own so deeply

Is it because the secret
Of our worthiness
And being loved
Is out
For one of us
Shared in public
Where it belongs

65. MY OWN BEST FRIEND

If I
Were my own
Very best friend

I would be
Available to myself
Happy for the time
We had with together

I would
Laugh even more

I would
Enjoy the sensuousness
Of nature
On walks
With myself
And my dog

I would
Share more of my pleasures
And treasures
With myself

I would
Introduce myself
To more of the things
Experiences and
People that intrigue me

I would value
My own preciousness

If I were
Truly
My own best friend
I would treat myself
Very well
And feel
Very blessed

What about you

66. REMEMBERING YOU

I'm happy for the time
We had together

I'm happy for moments
That we shared

I'm happy for the memories
You gave me

And the happiness
Of knowing that you cared

67. ADOLESCENT LONGING

We want to
Belong

And
Not

Be
Longing
For someone else

Or

Be
Longing to
Be
Someone else
So we can
Belong

We want
To belong
To someone

And someone
To belong
To us

Before too
Long

Goes bye

68. NOW

Dwell
Wallow
Breathe in
Swallow
The intense
Experience
Of this moment

Savor
The silent stillness

Letting go
Of commentary
Comparison
Thoughts and stories

Lose your mind
Let it slip away
For now
Enjoy the freedom
Of thoughtless
And mindless
Ease

Letting the beauty
Of now
Rush through you
And around you
Uninterrupted
Be timeless

Unhurried
And refreshed
In the joy of your senses

69. PARTLY DEPARTED

At a party
Sometimes it's hard
To avoid being
Where you are

You find
Yourself
Wanting to
Disappear
And still seem
Sincere
About wanting
To be there

Mentally
You try to leave
The party
Without taking
Your body with you

So
You have an out-of-body experience
Until you and your body
Can decide to stay there
Or be somewhere else
At the same time

70. HOW ARE YOU TREATED

Would you feel more
Loved
Appreciated
Encouraged
Valued

Would you feel more
Interesting
Clever
Talented
Capable
And worthy

If you treated
Yourself better

71. LOVING MOMENTS

In the middle
Of the night
Their faces
Appeared

Points of contact
When a sense of love
And caring was shared
If only for a moment
In time

On purpose
I dwelled
In this way
On playmates
Classmates
Those who shared lunch with me
Or walked with me
To school

Old crushes and lovers
Friends
And each family member

Those I wrote to
And called on the phone

Points of meeting
For the first time

Infatuation

A simple exchange of
Warm and friendly smiles

Those I worked
With and who grew close

I took time
To soak in these memories
Completely undistracted
By what happened
Later or where they were now

I stayed in love
Savoring each relationship
Filled
And overflowing
In the touching times
Of a lifetime of
Loving moments

72. INDWELLING POWER

I believed
Thoughts and feelings
Just appeared out of nowhere

I thought
I was a victim
Of my feelings

But later
I learned
I had an incredible power
To dwell on certain kinds
Of thoughts

Whatever thoughts
I dwelled on
Kept me feeling
The feeling
They created

I noticed
When I was sad
I was dwelling on
A lack
A loss
Or what I was missing

When I was fearful
Or angry
I was dwelling on
A threat
A potential attack
A vulnerability

And I discovered
When I was happy
I was dwelling
On gains and goals
Loves and loving

To selective a feeling
Select a thought
To change a feeling
Change a thought

To discover the source of my suffering
Was in my dwelling powers

I was no less important
Than the discovery of fire

It empowered me
And it will empowers you
To be happy

73. MOOD RINGS

Some of us know
About the rings

The kids wore them
'Cause they would change colors
Reflecting their mood

I was imagining
Mood rings
Of another kind
Colored smoke rings
Around our bodies
Moving outward
Showing us our mood
In colors

The warmth of our mood
Circling out
Like delicate vapor
Into a room

Or our darkened mood
Doing the same

We would see our mood
As others see it

Some of us would learn
To change our mood
For a better lighter one

After all
We would be rung
In public
By the color of our mood rings
Hard to ignore

And
When people gathered
We could see
The colors
Changing
As our own mood rings
Mixed
And we altered
Each other's mood
In rainbow filled rooms

74. SEEING-EYE CARS

It's 2014
The driverless car
Was coming
Toyota
Nissan
Mercedes
Have them now

What will it mean

Our lives would be changed

No more need for a license
We wouldn't be too old
Too young
Too disabled
To get where we wanted
To go

We would be safer

No more accidents
Lawyers suing us
The need for insurance
No more drunk-driving
Speeding
Or stealing cars remotely locked

Traveling would be a pleasure
We could take naps
Watch movies
Read
Use our phones
And computers

Car owning would be optional

Instead of our own car
We might just order it on demand
Automatically
From a nearby parking lot
Five minutes away

Let's see what happens
When seeing-eye cars
Drive better than we do

75. DISAPPEARING PROBLEM

I wonder
What would I do
If this wasn't a problem

I wonder
What would happen
If I took the problem
Out of this experience
I'm having

I wonder
If this problem
Is only a dramatic story
I'm making up

I wonder
Maybe
There is a gift
Hidden
In this problem

I wonder
Will it bring
A new resource
A new person
A source of help
Into my life

Hmmm
I wonder

76. DUST-BUNNY

TUMBLEWEEDS

Sometimes ideas
Collect in my mind
Like dust
Under the bed

Left too long
Dust-bunnies grow
In size
It's not wise
To leave them
There
Unattended

They gather
Weight and substance
Growing into tumbleweeds

That blow around the mind
Of a poet
During brainstorms
On dark nights

77. SLEEP

And Susan said

As I lie in bed
Listening to the
The worry and chatter
In my mind
Keeping me awake

I let it go on
For a while
And then I begin
To slow it down

And as it slows down
I begin to watch
As the words
Being said
Begin to appear
Before me
In large print
Coming off a ticker-tape
On a strip of white paper

As the words show up
I watch carefully
For the letter "O"
When an "O" appears
I see it as if it were

In the middle
Of the word G"O"D

And in wonder
I image the "O"
To be a large
Entry way
To a well-lit opening

And in God's presence
I enter the opening
Which leads me back
To my favorite
Beautiful
Safe
And peaceful place

There
I slowly
Take this all in
Through all my senses
And in this dwelling place
I rest in a comfortable spot
And fall asleep

78. HIDING FROM A FRIEND

The Monday Morning Ladies
A small group of very special friends
Who sewed and quilted and crocheted
Gathered today
At the art museum
To see a special display of flags

And placed among the many
American flags
Darla and Yoko noticed
The old Japanese flag

Darla told Yoko
She remembered the blackouts
During the War when she was very young
How a man came one night
And banged on the door
Of the family's home
Her grandparents were told
To lower the shades
And darken their lights

Yoko said
She too remembered the blackouts
On the other side of the world
In Japan

Darla said to her friend

There we were
Both of us
So many years ago
With our families just wanting to be safe
To go about our daily lives
With a roof over our heads and food to eat

It's fascinating
My friend
To discover
When we were both young
We shared an experience

We were both hiding in the dark
With our families
Thousands of miles apart
Because we were afraid
Of each other

So long before
We even met

79. A MESSAGE FROM THE ALIEN

It was a required seminar
About risk management
A real dozer of a topic
And one I knew well

The speaker was using
The old technology of the time
As he showed us his overheads
In the darkened room
I listened to the fan
Humming and numbing
In the background

By the second hour
As the presenter
Droned on and on
I began to drift into
A near-sleep

I tried to entertain myself
But
My head would nod-off
Awakening me

Then on the screen
Unnoticed by the speaker
A tiny little red ant appeared
To entertain me

Scampering among
The words on the transparency
Amused
I watched the ant scurry for a while
Then I thought maybe the bug
Was sending out a message
So I watched him carefully

I began writing down the sequence
Of the words
The little one touched
As he moved back and forth
Across the screen

He kept landing on
Four words

Don't
Unnecessary
Risks
Take

And there was the essence
Of the risk manager's message
Of the three hour presentation

Delivered
By the little alien
From another world
With humor
And precision

I had got the message
Now
With a clear conscience
I could fall asleep

80. THE OTHER ME

Through a painter's eyes
I now can see
The other me

The sun behind
Casts my shadowy silhouette
Ahead of me
So I follow
This other self as I walk

And as I run
It leads me
Faster

Until I turn
Retracing my steps
And heading
Toward the sun
My other self
Falls behind

Invisible
Until I turn my head
To see
If it remains still
Or follows me

And so it is
A shadowy self
Keeping me company

81. JULIE

People come into your life
In unexpected ways
When you need them

Love just shows up
In a form
Unrecognized at first

A softening force
A gentle pull
A generous source
Drawn into the lives
Who needed her

When the lives of others
Were falling apart
She held people together

With love in a place
A protected space
During stormy times
When "suppose tos"
Died

Julie
Was there
Standing and staying
For love in this family
That needed her

82. THE GIFT OF THE SHIFT

Our loving community
Advances

When we shift
Our focus

From finding enemies
And telling every one
How bad things are

To seeking out
Those who are doing good things
And helping them
Expand and multiply
The impact
Of their good works

83. THE GIFT

The 16th of May
Dorothy Pearl
Left us
Today

"They" said
She was slow
Retarded
But she was
Wise and kind-hearted
And caring

Shy at first
But she inched her way
Into your heart
With her gifts

For me
There were wonderful toys
Bop-it
Flashing guns
Dancing plastic plants
And books
About British royalty
She kept me informed
About Diana and Fergie

For others
So many thoughtful gifts

If there was a baby coming
Her crocheted-blanket
Was soon on its way
To the new arrival

By phone and letter
And playful presence
She was in your life

If you teased her
She smile
And joked about telling
Your mother
Or someone important

Today
She went Home
To see the mother
She had missed
For so long

Now
She's left us
Still blessed
By the gifts
Of her presence

84. TEACHERS AND TIME

Why do we remember
Our teachers
It was not as obvious
Until today

We spend six hours
Five days
A week
For most of the year
With them
At least in the early grades

They teach us
Tell us what's important
How to behave
And what we have to do
At home too
Preparing for the next day
We spend with them

In our childhood
Who gets more
Of our time
And has more influence
Than our teachers

No one

For they too
Are raisers
Of us
And our children

Without the credit
They deserve

85. SPIRITUAL WARRIORS

They were righteously
Indignant
Angry
At large corporate dragons
Poisoning and polluting
Our food supply

They would ruminate
Endlessly with each other
And with friends and family
Hoping to enlist them
In this holy war
And the sacred experience
Of rage

Those who
Would not be dragged
Into the trance
The obsession
The orgasm of outrage
Were accused
Of not caring

And pronounced guilty
Of lesser pursuits
The unholy practice
Of love and happiness

Losing sight
Of the dragon
Living in the mountainous cave
Unbelievers now became
The focus of the war
And the new inquisition

After all
What kind of
Witches and wizards
Would choose happiness
When they could be a
Righteously indignant
Spiritual warrior

86. MY WOUNDED ONES

I don't remember when it started
This attraction to wounded birds
And saving them

These women
All pretty
In their special way
And hurting
They would say
Indirectly

I loved them
And their wounds
Giving my life meaning
For a time
A long time

Until I learned
I could only offer
Company and comfort
But had no power
To heal
Their suffering

Powerless
To heal myself
Yet
Wizened by failure
Or was it surrender

To the Other Healer
Who could
Heal these
Precious
Wounded birds

87. THE THREE LEGGED DOG

He doesn't know
He cannot run

He doesn't know
He can't have fun

He doesn't know
How cruel his fate

He doesn't know
He cannot date

He doesn't know
He's different

He doesn't know
He's lost a leg

He doesn't know
He cannot beg

He doesn't know
He can't chase sticks

He doesn't know
He can't do tricks

He doesn't know
He should be sad

His doesn't know
It makes us glad
He doesn't know
He's different

88. CHRISTMAS PLANS

I was so lucky
You were my Dad

The only thing I regret
Was that last
Christmas
We did not spend together

I didn't say we would
So you made other plans
And I let you
Not insisting

I didn't know
We would never have
Another Christmas
Together

I'm sorry, Dad
But only for
A moment missed
'Cause I thought
We had forever

89. LET'S NOT DO LUNCH

When I offered a thought
She resisted it
Thinking
It did not suit her taste

Sometimes
Reluctantly
She would taste one
Chew on it
And spit it out

Presented in this form
She returned it
To me

When she offered
Her own tasty morsels
She expected them
To be taken in
Swallowed whole
Chewing and digestion
Unnecessary

Sharing thoughts
Eventually made us
Both
Sick with indigestion

So we stopped eating
Together

And sharing our
Food for thought

90. HEAVENLY BARRIERS

When I was a child
They told me God was up in Heaven
But I didn't know how to get there
I couldn't fly

They said I could go to Heaven
If I was very good
So I was

But then they told me
I couldn't go to Heaven
Until I was dead
So I've been waiting

I wonder
Why
They put God so far away

91. THE HOST

We enter new situations
Unconsciously praying
A friendly host
Will greet us
And connect us to potential friends
Show us around the place
Easing the way to contact

We wait for clues
That we are wanted
Hoping someone will
Let us into their lives
At least for a moment

We pray for a host
To overcome the awkwardness of meeting
To welcome us
Into the circle
We think is closed

We want to be invited in
Even if we
Turn down the invitation

Without an invitation
We hesitate
And wait
Unaware
We can answer
Our own prayer

And be the host
In our own lives
Without permission
Welcoming others
Inviting contact
And opening
To those around us

92. FIXING THE FAULTY FILTER

His filter
His mental filter
Was in backwards
Facing outward
Rather than inward

Screening in
What
Was better
Screened out

And screening out
What was better
Screened in

He saw darkness
Where there was light

Ugliness
Where there was beauty

Danger
Where there was love

He thought
The source of his disturbance
Was outside

Not inside
Until
The fault filter fixer
Fixed the faulty way
The filter faced

93. MORE COMMUNION

The more time
I spend in a moment
Of communion

The more
I experience
Tears of joy
And gratitude

The more
I notice the love
That surrounds me

The more amusing
I find the stories
The scary tales I tell
As I face the unknown
Thinking I must know
Rather than trust
In the outcome of change
Before it occurs

The more
I rest in
The quiet stillness of God

The more
I am in love with life

And those who
Surround me
And bless me
With their presence

94. GOING TO SCHOOL

He was the first child
Young and handsome
And at five
He was growing up
So fast

It was September
And his first day of school
Was approaching

He was excited about it
Having noticed
The large yellow school bus
That would
Pass through the neighborhood
The one with the big kids on it

He wanted to be a big kid too

His mother looked forward
To that day
With a mixture of relief
And sadness
A sign that he was leaving
If only for a couple hours a day

But he was pleased
So excited
And talking happily

About going to school

So the big day came
He was up early
And dressed and ready
At the bus stop
With his cute lunch box in hand

The bus arrived
The little guy
With mother's help
Got up the steps
Of the huge yellow bus
And off he went

Mother watched him
Disappear down the street

The morning of the next day
The little boy
Was sleeping in
So it was getting late

Mother went into his bedroom
And woke him saying
Come on it's time
To get dressed for school

The little boy looked puzzled
Mother said again
Come on it's time
To get dressed for school

The little boy said
But I already went to school
Yesterday

Confused
His mother
Paused a moment
Looked at him
And then smiled
Now understanding
His misunderstanding

95. HOLDING A GRUDGE

How does it feel
To hold a grudge

Is it uncomfortable
Painful
Prickly
To the touch

Does it hurt
Or pick at your open wounds
Leaving scars

What does a grudge
Whisper
Talk about
Or yell in your ear

And what does it say
That keeps people away

Why do we want
To hold a grudge
Anyway

It seems so unpleasant

96. REMINDERS

As a boy
I always loved smooth stones
Wonderful to feel
And keep in your pocket

In bookstores
I would notice The display
Of engraved rocks
In a basket

I would finger them
As I read the words
Peace
Gratitude
Serenity

Reminders

We don't seem
To need reminders
To feel badly

Who would buy
Stones that said
Anger
Regrets
Sadness
Panic

It's odd
We have to be reminded
To be happy

97. TAKING SIDES

My friend
Any friend of yours is a friend of mine
Any enemy of yours is an enemy of mine

Any enemy of your enemy is a friend of
yours
And is, therefore a friend of mine as well
Any friend of an enemy of yours is an
enemy of mine

We are friends together

Unless we become enemies
Then
Any friend of yours is an enemy of mine
And any enemy of yours is my friend
Any friend of mine will become your
enemy

And if
Somehow
We become friends
Again
Well
You know what happens then

I'm not sure how
We keep this up
Without high school
Family conflicts

And work situations

I wonder what would happen
If I chose
Not to have enemies

98. TEACHING KINDNESS

At first
I thought
She might be stuck
In the sadness
She noticed

She would say
It's soooo sad

And then
Describe a misunderstanding
She had witnessed

I thought
She was simply
Staying in her sorrow
Her disappointment
Her hurt

But
Knowing her
I suspended
My judgment
And listened

To what came
From her noticing
The source
Of her sadness

Not to wallow
In it

But to see
An opportunity
For kindness

And
When possible
To gently teach a way
Of opening to love
That might heal
The misunderstanding
And growing fear
That was separating
Family members
And friends

99. STAIN REMOVER

We now have wonderful
Spot removers
That make spots fade
And disappear
Renewing the beauty
Of what we see

I thought this gift
Could be applied
To the stain
Of unforgiveness
That falls on a certain relationship

Discoloring it
And making it ugly

What is this substance
We spill
On the relationship
But unmet
Perhaps unrealistic
Expectations

The stain it leaves
Remains untreated
For years

If only we could
Bring ourselves to
Pour the stain remover

On the spot
The expectation
That was never met

And watch it fade away

Removing the ugliness
We used to see

100. GOING HOME

I knew I was headed
Home
But feeling alone

I wondered
If anyone else
Was headed in that direction

I thought maybe
You were
And that we could
Walk together

I'd like your company

So walk with me
For a while

I'm going
Home
And not quite sure
How to get there

So as we walk
And as we talk
I'm sure
We'll pass the time

And as we get close
To the journey's
End
Maybe you'll
Be my friend
By then

And having walked
In the same direction

Maybe we'll discover
We live in the same house
And were brothers and sisters
All along
Going
Home
Together

ABOUT THE AUTHOR

DR. BOB WOODARD

Dr. Bob lives in Reno , Nevada, with his wonderful wife, Darla and his dog, Charlie Too. He is blessed by six children: Kim, Todd, Darla, Larry, Del and Angela, and their beautiful families. He has enjoyed writing short story poetry for decades and has fun, laughing, sharing, with a circle of friends and singing and playing the ukulele with his group called the Rubber Band.

He brings to his books a wisdom, humor, gentleness and humility that evolved from his interest in people, their troubles and a desire to find ways of reducing their personal suffering in the world. He spent a lifetime exploring the many, schools of psychotherapy and world religions. There he found answers in what he calls applied spirituality and psychology.

For most of his career, Dr. Bob was a licensed mental health professional with advanced degrees and studies in psychotherapy, marriage and family and spiritual counseling. He draws upon his work in over twenty-four different public and private settings. Currently, he has a practice as a life coach to professionals. In addition, he presents workshops on happiness, gratitude, and forgiveness, and conducts classes on A Course In Miracles and the Law of Attraction. He is dedicated to his own and the happiness of others at the deepest level.

He remains curious about how differently people think about and make sense of the world they see. He finds solace in the lighter side of life and is a keen observer of what makes people happy or unhappy.

MORE BOOKS FROM THE AUTHOR

If you enjoyed this book of short story poetry
by Dr. Bob Woodard,
you are sure to enjoy the paperbacks and
eBooks in the series called Secrets available at
Amazon Kindle.com Books.

SECRETS: *Things I Never Told You*

SECRETS II: *What I Left Unsaid*

SECRETS III: *There Is More I Must Tell You*

SECRETS V: *Living in Wonder*

SECRETS VI: *The Witness*

SOURCES OF INSPIRATION

Darla Woodard, Albert Woodard, Margaret Woodard, Kim Woodard Jankowiak, Todd Woodard, Richard Woodard, God, Susan Leedy, Nancy Jeppson, Sandy Tackett, Jim McCune, Dorothy Pearl, Donnie Townsend, A Course in Miracles, Helen Schucman, Bill Thetford, Center for Spiritual Living in Reno, digital technology, and the four emotions: fear, anger, sadness and happiness

PLEASE RATE THIS BOOK

I hope you will rate and review this book. If you like it your recommendation will help introduce the author and his writings to others, who will, in turn, enjoy and share it with others. It can also be given as a gift to those you love. Thank you! It has been my pleasure.